ATLAS OF THE EARTH

Illustrated by Daniel Moignot
Created by Gallimard Jeunesse
and Jean-Pierre Verdet

MOONLIGHT PUBLISHING / FIRST DISCOVERY ATLAS

Four billion years ago, our Earth
was probably just a ball of molten rock.

Over the next billion years the crust hardened
and the oceans filled. Eventually there was
one huge land mass surrounded by water.

The shapes of the oceans and continents
go on changing. You can see how
South America and Africa used to fit together.

This map shows the oceans and continents of the Earth.

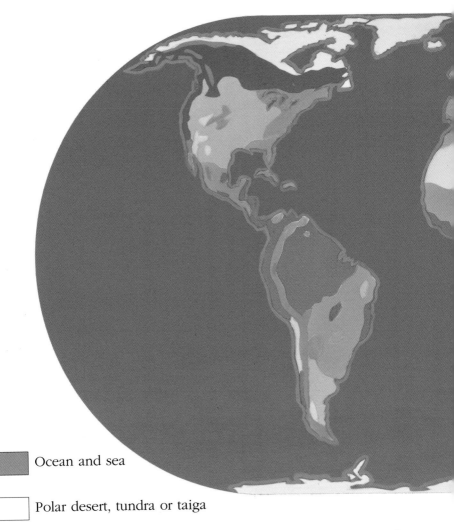

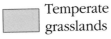

Ocean and sea

Polar desert, tundra or taiga

Mountain

Temperate grasslands

Tropical grasslands

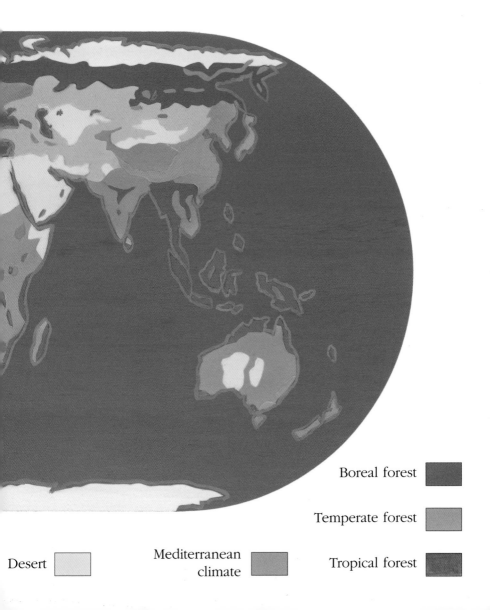

Boreal forest

Temperate forest

Desert

Mediterranean climate

Tropical forest

Two thirds of the Earth's surface
are covered with water.

Under water, the Earth's
shape is just as varied
as the landscape above.

There are plains,
hills and mountains.

The water in this mountain lake
is fresh water.

The water in the oceans is salt water.
The water in rivers and lakes is fresh water.

The water in the Dead Sea is very salty.
If you go swimming there, you will float easily.

At the end of the Ice Age,
deep valleys cut by
glaciers were flooded
with sea water.
Fjords were formed.

The sea batters the coastline all the time, changing its shape.

Coastlines may be rocky or sandy, mountainous or flat.

There are more than 500 active volcanoes on land. There are many more beneath the oceans.

Molten rock comes up
to the Earth's surface
from deep underground.

A volcanic eruption
under the sea can
make a new island!

Plants and animals
soon come to live on and
around the new island.

Open plains and forests stretch across
parts of North America and Europe.
Cereal crops are grown on good soil.

The steppes of Asia and the pampas
of South America are wide, flat plains too.
But the soil there is poor.

Some mountain
ranges, such as the European
Alps, are young. Wind and ice
have only just begun their work.

Other mountains
are much older.

Wind and weather
have eroded them.
They are more rounded.

Millions of years ago, the Colorado River
flowed gently across the flat lands
of the Colorado plateau.

As the plateau rose, the Colorado River tumbled more quickly to the sea. The river carved the Grand Canyon.

In Africa, grass plains stretch as far as
the eye can see. They are called the savannah.
They support vast numbers of animals.

Deserts are areas
where very little rain falls.

The Sahara Desert is so dry
that humans cannot live there.

The North Pole is in
the frozen Arctic Ocean.
The Inuit people live in the
lands around the Arctic Ocean.
Polar bears, seals, walruses and
reindeer also live here.